Mississippi

A Buddy Book
by
Julie Murray

ABDO
Publishing Company

VISIT US AT

www.abdopub.com

Published by ABDO Publishing Company, 4940 Viking Drive, Edina, Minnesota 55435.

Copyright © 2006 by Abdo Consulting Group, Inc. International copyrights reserved in all countries. No part of this book may be reproduced in any form without written permission from the publisher. Buddy Books™ is a trademark and logo of ABDO Publishing Company.

Printed in the United States.

Edited by: Sarah Tieck
Contributing Editor: Michael P. Goecke
Graphic Design: Deb Coldiron, Maria Hosley
Image Research: Sarah Tieck
Photographs: BrandX, Clipart.com, Corel, Creatas, Getty Images, Library of Congress, Mississippi Development Authority/Division of Tourism (photograph on page 15), One Mile Up, Photodisc, Photos.com

Library of Congress Cataloging-in-Publication Data

Murray, Julie, 1969-
    Mississippi / Julie Murray.
        p. cm. — (The United States)
    Includes index.
        Contents: A snapshot of Mississippi — Where is Mississippi? — All about Mississippi — Cities and the capital — Famous citizens — Plantations — Mississippi Petrified Forest — Gulf Island National Seashore — A history of Mississippi.
    ISBN 1-59197-683-9
        1. Mississippi—Juvenile literature. I. Title.

F341.3.M87 2005
976.2—dc22

2005043334

Table Of Contents

A Snapshot Of Mississippi

Mississippi has white sand beaches, lush forests, rolling hills, and rich farmland. But, when most people think of Mississippi, they think of a river. The state got its name from the Mississippi River. Mississippi is a Native American word that means "great waters."

There are 50 states in the United States. Every state is different. Every state has an official state nickname. Mississippi is sometimes called "The Magnolia State." This is because of the state's blooming magnolia trees.

Magnolia blossoms

Barges and boats carry goods along the Mississippi River.

Mississippi became the 20th state on December 10, 1817. It is the 32nd-largest state in the United States. It has 47,695 square miles (123,529 sq km) of land. Mississippi is home to 2,844,658 people.

Where Is Mississippi?

There are four parts of the United States. Each part is called a region. Each region is in a different area of the country. The United States Census Bureau says the four regions are the Northeast, the South, the Midwest, and the West.

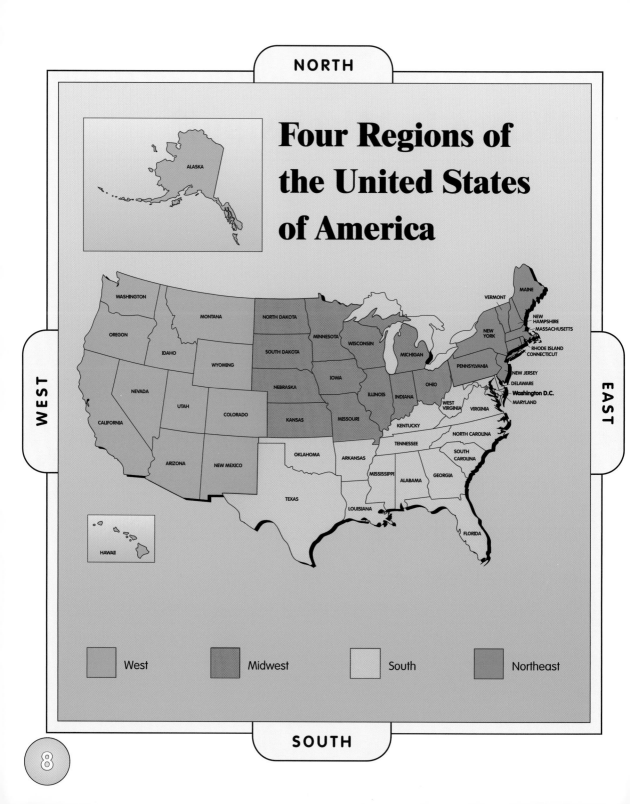

Four Regions of the United States of America

WEST

EAST

ALASKA

WASHINGTON
MONTANA
NORTH DAKOTA
OREGON
IDAHO
MINNESOTA
WISCONSIN
SOUTH DAKOTA
WYOMING
MICHIGAN
NEVADA
UTAH
COLORADO
NEBRASKA
IOWA
ILLINOIS
INDIANA
OHIO
CALIFORNIA
KANSAS
MISSOURI
VERMONT
MAINE
NEW HAMPSHIRE
MASSACHUSETTS
NEW YORK
RHODE ISLAND
CONNECTICUT
PENNSYLVANIA
NEW JERSEY
DELAWARE
Washington D.C.
MARYLAND
WEST VIRGINIA
VIRGINIA
KENTUCKY
NORTH CAROLINA
TENNESSEE
ARIZONA
NEW MEXICO
OKLAHOMA
ARKANSAS
SOUTH CAROLINA
MISSISSIPPI
ALABAMA
GEORGIA
TEXAS
LOUISIANA
FLORIDA

HAWAII

West   Midwest   South   Northeast

Cotton is grown in Mississippi on large farms.

Mississippi is in the South region of the United States. It is part of an area that is called the Deep South. Mississippi's weather is hot and humid much of the year.

Mississippi is bordered by four other states and a body of water. Tennessee lies to the north. Alabama is to the east. The Mississippi River creates the state's western border with Arkansas and Louisiana. The Gulf of Mexico lies to the south of Mississippi.

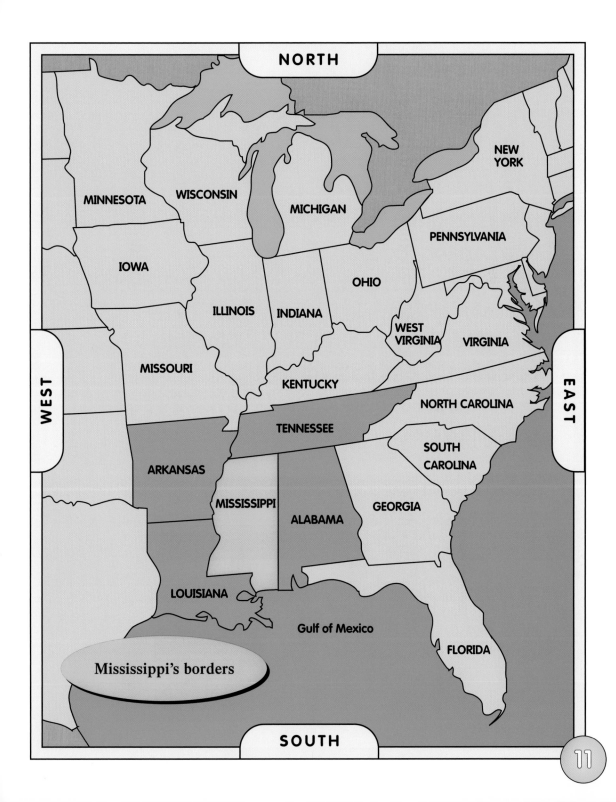

NORTH

WEST

EAST

SOUTH

NEW YORK

MINNESOTA

WISCONSIN

MICHIGAN

PENNSYLVANIA

IOWA

OHIO

ILLINOIS

INDIANA

WEST VIRGINIA

VIRGINIA

MISSOURI

KENTUCKY

TENNESSEE

NORTH CAROLINA

ARKANSAS

SOUTH CAROLINA

MISSISSIPPI

ALABAMA

GEORGIA

LOUISIANA

Gulf of Mexico

FLORIDA

Mississippi's borders

Mississippi

State abbreviation: MS

State nickname: The Magnolia State

State capital: Jackson

State motto: *Virtute et armis* (Latin for "By valor and arms")

Statehood: December 10, 1817, 20th state

Population: 2,844,658, ranks 31st

Land area: 47,695 square miles (123,529 sq km), ranks 32nd

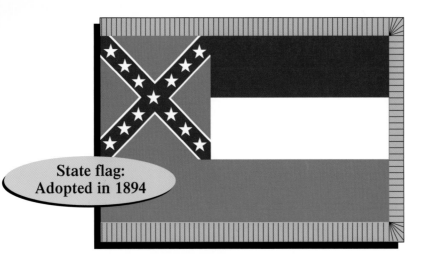

State flag:
Adopted in 1894

State song: "Go, Mis-sis-sip-pi"

State government: Three branches: legislative, executive, and judicial

Average July temperature: 81°F (27°C)

Average January temperature: 46°F (8°C)

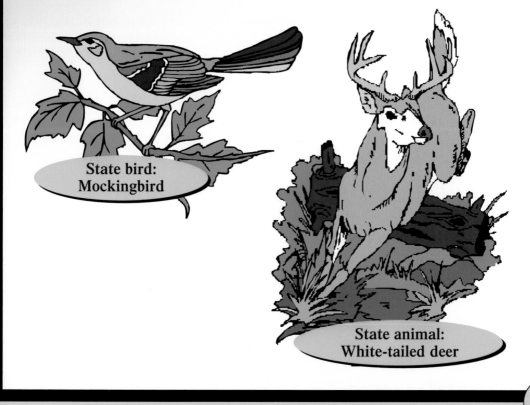

State flower: Magnolia

State bird: Mockingbird

State animal: White-tailed deer

Cities And The Capital

Jackson is the capital city of Mississippi. It is also the largest city in the state. Jackson is in the center of the state. It is located on the Pearl River. It is sometimes called the "Crossroads of the South."

The capitol building in Jackson.

Gulfport is the second-largest city and Biloxi is the third-largest city. They are very close together. Along with Pascagoula, they make a large metropolitan area. These three cities are located on the shores of the Gulf of Mexico.

Famous Citizens

Elvis Presley (1935–1977)

Elvis Presley was born in Tupelo in 1935. He was very poor when he was growing up. As an adult, he was famous for his music. Many people remember him as the "King of Rock and Roll." He is known for hit songs such as "Hound Dog," "Jailhouse Rock," and "Blue Suede Shoes." Presley also acted in more than 30 movies.

Elvis Presley

Famous Citizens

Oprah Winfrey (1954–)

Oprah Winfrey was born in Kosciusko in 1954. She is a famous talk-show host, actress, and business-woman. She is the host of *The Oprah Winfrey Show*. This is one of the most popular shows on television.

Oprah Winfrey

Plantations

Plantations are part of the history of Mississippi. In the 1800s, there were plantations all over the south. A plantation is a large farm that usually only grows one crop. Cotton was a main crop that was grown on plantations.

A cotton plant.

In order to run a plantation there needed to be a lot of workers. Slaves worked on the plantations. The American Civil War helped free the slaves. The end of slavery caused the end of many southern plantations.

A plantation house in Mississippi.

Today, people can still visit many of the old plantations in Mississippi. They can see the beautiful houses where plantation owners lived. They can also see the small shacks the slaves lived in.

Mississippi Petrified Forest

The Mississippi Petrified Forest isn't actually a forest. It was created by the remains of trees. They broke apart and were carried there by a flooded river. This happened more than 36 million years ago.

The logs were once like living trees. But, over millions of years they turned to rock. Today, people come to see the unusual formations. They also come to see how big the trees were. Some were more than 100 feet (30 m) tall.

This wood is petrified.

Gulf Islands
National Seashore

The Gulf Islands National Seashore is a string of small islands that stretch for 160 miles (258 km). Gulf Islands National Seashore runs from Cat Island in Mississippi to Santa Rosa Island in Florida. Some of the islands are about 10 miles (16 km) off the coast of Mississippi.

The Gulf Islands National Seashore includes salt marshes, bayous, forests, bright blue waters, and snow white beaches. Two islands in Mississippi are wilderness areas. These are Horn Island and Petit Bois Island.

Hermit crabs can be found in
Mississippi's marshes.

Ferries carry people and vehicles from shore to shore.

People can take a ferry from Gulfport to West Ship Island. There, people can visit historic Fort Massachusetts.

The Gulf Island National Seashore is home to the great blue heron (top) and the brown pelican (bottom).

Mississippi

1540: Hernando de Soto explores Mississippi.

1817: Mississippi becomes the 20th state on December 10.

1861: Mississippi says it is no longer part of the United States. The American Civil War begins.

Medgar Evers

1863: Union troops win the Battle of Vicksburg. This means Mississippi and other Southern states lose control of the Mississippi River.

1870: Mississippi rejoins the United States.

1898: Edward Adolf Barq Sr. invents root beer in Biloxi.

1907: Boll weevils destroy Mississippi's cotton crop.

1962: James Meredith is the first African American to attend the University of Mississippi.

Workers had to pull the boll weevils off the cotton.

1963: Civil rights leader Medgar Evers is shot and killed in Jackson.

1964: Dr. James D. Hardy performs the first heart transplant surgery in Jackson. He put the heart of a chimpanzee into a human man.

2001: Citizens vote to keep the 1894 state flag.

Cities in Mississippi

Tupelo

Greenville

Kosciusko

Vicksburg

Meridian

★ Jackson

Hattiesburg

Gulfport Biloxi

Pascagoula

Important Words

American Civil War the United States War between the Northern and the Southern states.

bayou an area with soft, wet land, and slow-moving water.

capital a city where government leaders meet.

civil rights rights for all citizens.

humid air that is damp or moist.

nickname a name that describes something special about a person or a place.

plantation a large farm that grows only one crop.

slave a person who is bought and sold as property.

Web Sites

To learn more about Mississippi, visit ABDO Publishing Company on the World Wide Web. Web site links about Mississippi are featured on our Book Links page. These links are routinely monitored and updated to provide the most current information available.

www.abdopub.com

Index